COMING
ON
CHRISTMAS

Spiritual and *Real-Life Inspiration*
for Those with Too Much to Do
During the Month of December

JUDITH COPELAND

D0910783

Coming On Christmas: Spiritual and Real-Life Inspiration for Those with Too Much to Do During the Month of December

Published by Norway Hill Publishing, Hancock, New Hampshire

Paperback ISBN: 978-1-7334117-0-7

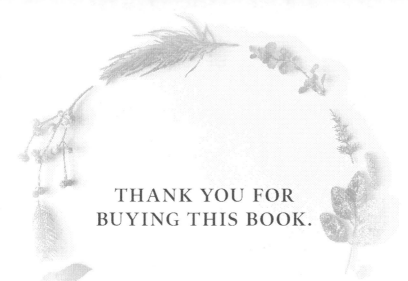

THANK YOU FOR
BUYING THIS BOOK.

As a thank you for investing in this book, I would like to offer you an extra resource for deepening your experience during the Christmas season.

Click *here* to get your copy of my December Guide.

Also, please know that a portion of the sale proceeds from this book will go to End 68 Hours of Hunger, an organization that sends home food each week with children who are food insecure so that they will not go hungry over the weekend.

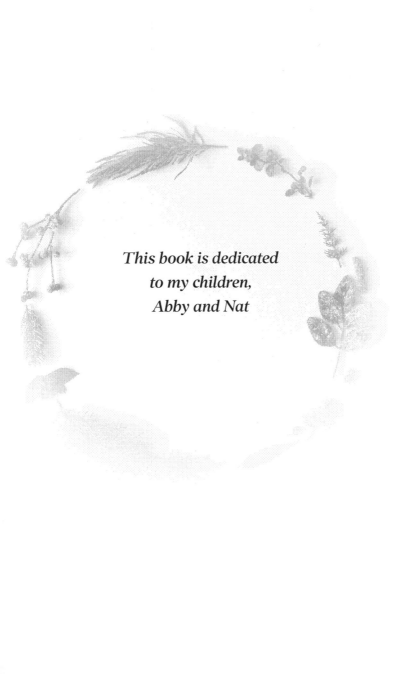

*This book is dedicated
to my children,
Abby and Nat*

CONTENTS

INTRODUCTION

This is a book for those who make Christmas for others. It's a book for those who wish their own experience of the weeks leading up to Christmas had a stronger spiritual chord but aren't sure how to achieve that and don't have the time to figure it out.

For many of us, the month of December begins with a sense of possibility. Our creativity kicks in and we dream big about Christmas. But before too long, this exuberance may be eclipsed by a sense of panic. There are so many things to do, but the unexpected has an uncanny way of making an appearance. Illness, grief, loneliness, a sense of inadequacy when we compare ourselves to those who seem to have it all together—I've felt all those things during the Christmas season. What I've learned is that it may take some paring down and reprioritizing to arrive at a sense of peace. We may have to learn to wait things out or to live more fully in the moment, even when it's not one of our choosing. The readings in this book loosely follow that progression—Possibility, Panic, Paring Down, and Peace.

In an ideal world, we would all want the weeks before Christmas (Advent, as these four weeks are called on the Christian liturgical calendar) to be a special, stand-alone season with its own themes and rhythms. A time to dive deeply into the traditional spiritual themes of waiting and judgment.

But if your life is anything like mine, things aren't so neatly ordered. My life is more like a big, messy notebook with everything scribbled down side by side—seasons, ideas, people, and projects bleeding into one another. Christmas jumps all over Advent and vice versa.

Over time, I've come to be okay with that. I don't believe it's a lack of discipline on my part or an inability to stand up to the juggernaut of Christmas commercialism or a backing away from some of the harder, eschatological messages of Advent. It's just the way life lived in a diverse, multigenerational community of family, friends, and parishioners unfolds.

This is a book for those who love Advent and Christmas, but also find themselves overwhelmed by all the demands that the month of December places on them. Using the biblical story, examples from my own life, and Christmas traditions from the past, this book celebrates the season's unexpected joys and sorrows. It claims its wonders and surprises, even when they do roll out in one jumbled, untidy mess. Wasn't that the way things unfolded around that first Christmas, so long ago in Bethlehem?

DECEMBER 1:

THE CHRISTMAS MAKER'S CLUB

When I was in my twenties, I stood in awe of people who were "settled," whose addresses didn't change from year to year, whose books lived in proper bookcases, who had artwork in real frames and not just posters and geological survey maps thumbtacked to the wall, and who had put together carefully curated collections of things.

One December, early in my ministry, I was invited to the home of one of my mentors, a pastor in a nearby town. I suppose she had a Christmas tree with tasteful white lights, beeswax candles, and the balsam wreath that one might expect in a Connecticut parsonage, but what I remember was her collection of antique Christmas books set out throughout the house, beautifully bound books from the late 19th and early 20th centuries. The stories were sentimental, the authors long forgotten, but the bindings were works of art. I was hooked, and I, too, became a collector. For the next two decades, I would haunt used bookstores (and later eBay) and, with a budget of no more than ten dollars per book, slowly put together a collection of my own.

One of my favorites is a volume from 1908 by the Maine author Edith A. Sawyer called "The Christmas Makers Club." It's the story of three girls who, finding themselves bored, form a secret club they call "The Christmas Makers Club." They meet weekly, and with the help of an adult neighbor, sew doll clothes and make other Christmas gifts for the children who live in a nearby convalescent home. Sometimes, Ben, the twin brother of one of the girls joins them, for he, too, is handy with needle and thread. The book has strong, graphic illustrations, but it's the title I love best—"The Christmas Makers Club."

Many of us take on the role of being Christmas Makers. We bake the cookies and organize the cookie swaps and carol sings. We transport children to pageant and choir rehearsals and soothe the hurt feelings of the ones who are perennially cast as shepherds and never get to play Mary or Joseph. We choose (and sometimes cut down) Christmas trees and wrestle them into poorly engineered tree stands. We stay up late at night thinking up brilliant gift ideas, and then we stay up even later wrapping them. We turn donated sheets into angel costumes and dollar store garlands into haloes. We go to parties we're much too exhausted to enjoy. We keep an ear to the ground for neighbors who may be alone. We engage our children in acts of kindness for others, even though it would be easier to do the shopping for Toys for Tots by ourselves. We keep family traditions alive and practice tolerance when members of our extended families come together. We make Christmas for others.

But sometimes, all that Christmas making wears us out. We arrive at Christmas day exhausted and spent, wondering if it's really worth it. Some will tell us to cut back, to practice better self-care. But what if being a "Christmas Maker" is part of our core identity, something that, even when it pushes us to exhaustion, we truly enjoy? I'm willing to wear myself out on things that matter, to overdo for a good cause. Christmas making for others makes me deeply happy.

But it is also important to keep things in perspective. Ben, that proto-feminist brother who sews in Sawyer's story, initially chides his sister and her friends for calling themselves "The Christmas Makers." As he so wisely reminds them, none of us can "make Christmas." In all the important ways, it has already been made once upon a time in a town called Bethlehem.

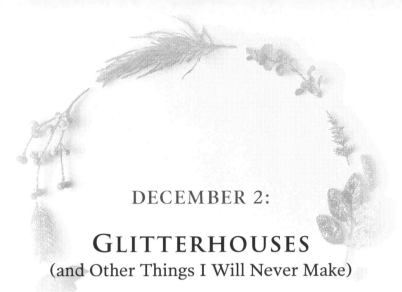

DECEMBER 2:

GLITTERHOUSES
(and Other Things I Will Never Make)

Every year, usually early in December, I think to myself that this is the year I'm going to do it. This is the year that I'm going to make a glitterhouse. Or two of three. Or maybe a whole village.

If you don't know what glitterhouses are, they're tiny, often ornately decorated cardboard houses used as Christmas decorations. Their name comes from the fact that they are often heavily doused in fine glitter—the kind that sparkles like new-fallen snow.

Sometimes they're called putz houses, from the German word meaning "to put" or, more colloquially, "to putter." Families with collections of glitterhouses would, at Christmastime, "putz" or putter around with them, arranging them on the mantel or around the tree, often as part of a toy train set-up.

The first glitterhouses were made from candy boxes, while the heyday for the commercially available ones began in 1928. Japan provided hundreds of different models for export. Although their popularity had waned by the 1960s, today, they're a DIY favorite with templates widely available on the Internet.

I'm not sure what the appeal of glitterhouses is for me. Maybe it's the appeal of miniatures, that delight many people seem to take in small things. Or maybe it's the appeal of the house motif. There is nostalgia and a sense of stability conveyed in the image of a house or home. It doesn't matter if it resembles my house; any simple house with clean lines will do. Home sweet home.

Or maybe it's that I'm under the impression that making a glitterhouse is doable. It doesn't require special skills, just a little cutting with an Exacto knife, a little painting and gluing, and then the fun part, pouring on the glitter. It's probably born of false confidence, but I am certain that I could make a glitterhouse.

But somehow, I never do. I've gotten as far as searching out the right kind of glitter and downloading a template from the Internet, but never any further. All the other Christmas things press in, and glitterhouses eventually drop off my to-do list.

But I love the little surge of inspiration that comes just from thinking about glitterhouses. That buzz of creativity and projected accomplishment. And I know I'm not alone. Christmas brings out the wannabe Maker in many of us, even if we're not especially artistic, crafty, or inclined in that direction.

Maybe it's okay not to get around to all the projects we dream about. Having something we want to do but haven't gotten to yet is one of the ways we spin out a future.

In the Christian church, the season of Advent is all about the future, or eschatology, to use the theological word for a sacred future. Traditional Advent devotionals draw on texts from the prophets of Ancient Israel, men like Jeremiah and Isaiah, whose raison d'être was to invoke the future of Israel.

Sometimes, the little things we dream about are connected to our bigger dreams. My glitterhouse fantasies may be silly, but they're one of the ways I think about a future. The future I dream of is one where all God's children are sheltered and where everyone feels at home, in their own skin and in their own communities.

DECEMBER 3:

MAKING LISTS

It's no wonder that there's a census in the Christmas story. Yes, it's the plot device that gets Mary and Joseph to the prophetically prescribed spot for their son's birth, but it has come down to us as an important detail in the telling of the story. Most are familiar with the abridged version of the story in Luke's gospel, which begins with a census:

In those days a decree went out from Emperor Augustus that all the world should be registered. This was the first registration and was taken while Quirinius was governor of Syria.

A census is a list. And if your Christmas is anything like mine, it runs on lists. Of course, for the sake of full disclosure, I should say that even out of season, I'm an inveterate list maker: contact lists, grocery lists, list of books to read, and lists of books I have read. Open my planner and every few pages, you're likely to find some kind of list.

But in December, my list-making game takes a big uptick. I have lists of presents purchased, lists of gift ideas, lists of people to send cards to, lists of shut-ins to visit, playlists of Christmas music, lists of holiday recipes to try, lists of things that would be "fun to do." Okay, we're not flying to Asheville to see the National Gingerbread House Competition or going skating at Rockefeller Center, but a sleigh ride and hot chocolate around a fire in the New Hampshire woods may just be possible.

Marilyn McEntyre, another self-professed list maker, and author of the book *Making a List: How a Simple Practice Can Change Our Lives and Open Our Hearts*, reminds us that lists are mirrors, and that they show us "something about what has come to matter to us." In times of personal loss, a to-do list "might be a lifeline, keeping you connected to daily life when grief threatens to overwhelm. Or in times of celebration, it could be a space for imagining ways to make love visible."But perhaps McEntyre's insight that I appreciate most is her observation that list making slows us down. This stands in contrast to the way I've always thought of lists as things that get dashed off, scribbled down as quickly as possible, a way of capturing the ideas in my head. The brain dump is what one list guru calls it.

And that's the way the process works, at least for the first few items on any list. But after that, if I were to watch a hidden camera video of myself making a list, I bet McEntyre would be proven right. List making gets more thoughtful, more introspective, and yes, a little harder, as you go along.List making can be a form of meditation. It's a way of emptying the mind, of letting the page receive the weight and relieve the mental pressure of all the things I think I need to do. But it's also a way of filling the heart, of sifting through my competing loyalties, priorities, and points of inspiration. It's a way of getting to the essential core of things.

To get in the mood, I put on some music, pour a cup of coffee or a glass of wine (depending on the time of day), grab my favorite pen, and, in my best handwriting, begin my master Christmas list. Eventually, it may branch off into a series of more specialized lists: cards, presents, baking, etc. But that comes later.

One of my favorite lists centers on the kind of Christmas experience that each of the people in my inner circle need in any particular year. Even within a family, Christmas is not one-size-fits-all. The high school senior who will be spending the holiday struggling over procrastinated college applications is in a different place from the mother-to-be who is contentedly pregnant. And the up and coming young professional who has just received a big promotion and a pay raise that will enable her to clear her student loan debt is not where her sixty-year-old father may be, with downsizing in the wind at his company and rumors that his department is in the crosshairs. The grandmother who has lost her husband, the last of her siblings, and her best friend in the past calendar year may be sharing space on the sofa with an exuberant six-year-old who is certain he just heard the reindeer on the roof. It's amazing how many different Christmases there are just in one family.

My list looks something like this. I write down the name of the person. And then I jot down a few notes about what may be on their heart this year. The good and the bad. Sometimes, I'm just guessing (and in my somewhat reserved New England family, that's often the case), but it doesn't matter. I've learned to trust my intuition and rely on God to fill in the blanks.

Next, I start listing the things that could be done to help sweeten the season for each of "my people" individually:

- a moratorium on nagging about laundry and room cleaning,
- a compliment,
- flowers or an invitation to lunch on a date when an anniversary of loss comes up,
- a voluntary cutback on holiday spending,
- a box of pregnancy tea,
- an invitation to take a walk,
- comfort food dropped off on the porch without imposing the obligation of conversation, or
- a couple of photos not emailed as attachments but printed out and placed in hand.

Lists remind us of the particulars. Just as Mary and Joseph's family had to be enumerated, so too do the needs and desires of our beloveds. We can save our gifts and gestures for that glut of goodwill that overwhelms everyone on Christmas morning, but if we make our lists early on, we'll find there are things we can do all month long to remind the people we love of our commitment to their wellbeing.

DECEMBER 4:

ON THE SUBJECT OF CHRISTMAS CARDS

O verheard at the next table, as I eavesdropped shamelessly on a pair of millennials meeting for coffee:

Did you see Carrie's Christmas card?

Yeah, wasn't it amazing? How does she do that?

The plaid-shirt-at-the-Christmas-tree-farm theme was great.

Totally Insta-worthy.

They must have done that photoshoot back in the fall.

Do you know who she hired?

I think Elegant Images, but you have to book them a couple of months out.

Have you ordered your cards yet?

No. I didn't get it together to get a good photo of every-one this year. We may not send any.

Silence.

And on my part, sympathy.

It used to be that sending Christmas cards meant going to the stationary store, taking ten minutes to pick out a box of pleasing cards, and then coming home and addressing them. Sending out Christmas cards didn't include the prerequisites of dressing and herding family members into a photo shoot, spending late night sessions in front of a computer monitor, fiddling around with the templates provided by the printing companies, and laboring to compose a message that sets just the right tone in the prescribed number of characters—newsy, but not too braggy. The heavy burden of all that prep work makes me miss the mass-produced manger scenes and pine trees in the snow.

Sending Christmas cards is a good thing, but it should be done in the spirit of making a real connection. God reached across the time-space continuum (and probably a few dimensions that we don't even know about) to connect with us through the Christ child. *Connection* should be our mantra for the month. It's all about connection.

However, there's more than one way to connect. Send out a hundred cards and make people glad (or jealous) with Photoshopped family photos or entertain them with the funny outtakes. Or write just one card to the person on your list who most needs to get one.

A few years ago, I created a template for writing a more meaningful Christmas card, and I've received requests for it ever since. It takes time to write a message like this, but even if you never get around to sending the card, it's also a good way to hold someone in prayer.

You begin by thinking about the person you want to connect with—how long you've known them, how you came to know them, and what the nature of your relationship has been, whether measured in weeks or in decades. People come into our lives at different times and in different seasons. Each entry point is to be honored.

The first thing you may want to share with them is something recalled. Is there a particular memory that sums up your connection with them? It's amazing how powerful sharing a particular memory can be and how much that sharing can mean to another person. Many of us downplay our own importance to others, and we don't realize the impact of some little thing we may have said or done. If you could tell only one story about your friendship with this person, what would that story be? Put it into words.

Secondly, offer something revealed. Tell a secret. Is there something about yourself that you've never shared? Or perhaps this person has influenced you in some way that you may never have put into words. Relationships grow when we take risks. Saying something that you've never gotten around to saying may feel risky, and perhaps a little awkward, but it's one of the ways that friendships deepen.

Finally, lift up something revered. When we revere something, it involves both respect and awe. What do you most appreciate, admire, or cherish about this person or about your relationship with them? In one sentence, what do you treasure most?

Too often, we leave these things unspoken.

We assume that the other person knows how we feel. And maybe they do. Or maybe not. Best to be explicit about it while we can, before it's too late. Over the years, especially in my role as a pastor, but also as a family member and friend, I can't tell you how many times I've heard people in moments of great distress say how much they wished they had taken the time to tell someone how much that person meant to them when they had the chance. Conversely, it has been my privilege to have people pull out treasured letters or show me emails and texts in which someone has done exactly that. Few things mean more to another person than to hear that they have mattered.

Something recalled, something revealed, something revered. That's my recipe if you want to write the kind of Christmas card that people will keep and read over and over.

DECEMBER 5:

THE IMPROV ACT

Creativity is part of the Christmas story. But it's not just the creativity of making things. It's the creativity of making things work, of taking whatever rolls your way and making sense of it. The creativity of Christmas is the creativity of improvisation. And it would seem that improv is woven into the original story.

I like to imagine Joseph walking into the stable and immediately starting to rearrange things, moving the manger and the milking stools to make it as comfortable a labor and delivery room as possible for Mary. It's the creativity of making the space work. It's not so different from the creativity called upon when we're trying to figure out how to house our holiday guests. Soothing the children who will be displaced from their rooms. Moving rugs and furniture so the frail elderly who are coming to stay won't slip. Sometimes, creativity expresses itself in the way we make space for people.

I like to imagine the magi, packing for their epic journey, debating what gifts they might bring, and then what they would put them in. A silver box inlaid with lapis lazuli or maybe a hand-carved ebony casket? Of course, this is pure conjecture, but I think of the magi and their presentation skills every time I receive a gift from someone so beautifully wrapped that it seems like an affront to open it. Sometimes creativity expresses itself in the way we deliver things.

Most of all, I like to imagine the shepherds, looking at the night sky and identifying the constellations. Perhaps testing their eyesight, as you do when you try to see distant stars. But then comes the great interruption— the dazzling new star that broke out of all previously known patterns of sky and light. I think of the shepherds every time someone I know gets news that rearranges all their previously known routines. Sometimes, creativity expresses itself as we try to make sense of the emerging patterns in our lives.

Creativity sometimes means being a maker, but other times, it means making do or re-creating something out of the things that fly our way unexpectedly, the things that come out of the blue. 'Tis the season of improvisation.

DECEMBER 6:

CRAMMING IT ALL IN

I drive a fifteen-mile roundtrip to do basic errands like go to the bank, gas up my car, or shop for grocery staples, but only need to drive a quarter of a mile up the hill to our local Christmas tree farm. So, the excursion "to cut down our own Christmas tree" hardly counts as an excursion. But during the years before I moved here, it did and finding a window of time when everyone in the family was free and the cut-your-own places were open seemed impossible to pin down.

Of course, it didn't help that we were trying to squeeze it in-between all the other Christmas activities we wanted to do. Our list, which probably was typical for a middle-class family, included school plays and holiday concerts (at one point, three children at three different schools, plus a last minute scramble for clarinet reeds), visits with grandparents who lived in other states, the church Christmas pageant and its schedule of rehearsals, gingerbread house making, three or four Yankee swaps (each requiring its own clever gift), cookie exchanges requiring dozens of homemade cookies (and let's face it, those who attended the exchanges didn't want the messy ones my kids decorated), nursing home visits with the Girl Scouts, and because Boston was the setting for the holidays of my own childhood, I often pushed for a trip to the city to see the Nutcracker, the Black Nativity, the Christmas Revels, or maybe just the lights on Boston Common. We did too much, and we often paid the price. By Christmas morning, we were nearly catatonic.

Looking back, it seems so simple. Why did I think that every Christmas had to include every possible holiday experience? Why did I insist on cramming them all in, of mainlining every blessed Christmas activity I could think of? We had Carpe Diem Christmases, to be sure, but I doubt that's what we needed.

An older and wiser me would have asked everyone in the family to tell me what ONE thing mattered most to them that year. I would have left more space in-between, more room to breathe, more room to savor, more room for each of the experiences we were having to really sink in and gather meaning. Yes, it would have been hard to say "no" to some of the things that we were "expected" to do, but I can say with confidence that Christmas still would have happened. Christmas always happens. The Christ child gets born, and born again each year, with or without perfect piping on the gingerbread people.

THE CURSE OF ALWAYS

The word *always* has to be one of the curses of the English language and one that carries disproportionate weight at Christmas time. Tradition can be beautiful, but it also can be a heavy burden. Once an "always" gets attached to something, it may take delicate surgery to remove it.

I think of the couples negotiating their first Christmases together and, even more poignantly, the children in blended families trying to find their way. They may hold onto their own bit of Christmas turf, not to mention family identity, by pronouncing, maybe with a bit of an edge, "In my family, we *always*..."

For others, the always is something we hear in our heads. We promulgate ancestral expectations whenever we remember the long list of things that our loved ones always did. Maybe your mother always made Christmas outfits for all her children. Or she baked 14 different kinds of Christmas cookies. Took everyone skiing on Christmas Eve. Selected a special book for each child and inscribed them with thoughtful, personalized messages. Strung popcorn and cranberries. Decorated an outside tree for the birds. Took shifts ringing the Salvation Army bell. Participated in a Messiah sing. Made scarves and hats for the homeless. Was a secret Santa to a family in town. Helped elderly neighbors put up and take down their Christmas trees. Blew a month's food budget on a rib roast. Went out to the swamp and cut winterberries to decorate window boxes. Made her own wrapping paper with potato prints. Spent a whole day setting up her collection of creches, snow globes, or nutcrackers.

But your mother's traditions may not be your own. And just because you inherited her Dickens Village, doesn't mean you have to put it out. If it's not your thing, if it doesn't add meaning, or in Marie-Kondo-speak, "spark joy," then don't be seduced by the "always" that got attached to it somewhere along the way. Maybe you're not an arranger and would rather take to the woods for the afternoon.

All our Christmas traditions are ephemeral. Beyond the stories we have in Luke and Matthew's Gospels, everything else is "extra." Our so-called traditions, hallowed as they may be, are all overlays. And it's surprising how easily they can be lifted and replaced.

But if phrases like "My mother always..." or "In my family, we always..." still haunt you and make you feel guilty, then try to figure out a way to honor the tradition in spirit, to give thanks for what it may have meant to your family over the years. This may take the form of an imagined conversation that begins by lifting up the tradition that's going on sabbatical or being mothballed, and addressing the ancestral spirits:

Mom, I'm not going to do XXX this year.

I thank you for all the years you did it, because it taught me XXX.

I honor that teaching by remembering it, and I carry it forward in the spirit of what it meant to you.

It sounds a little artificial, and may feel awkward and stilted, but you will be surprised by how liberating this little ritual can be. There comes a time to let go of those things with the "always" tag. Things that have become yours or landed on your shoulders, but that you never fully took on as your own. Goodbye, ancestral expectations. Goodbye, things that eat up your energy and keep you from celebrating Christmas in a way that's expressive of your own spirit.

LETTING PEOPLE DOWN

At some point in December, the vise begins to tighten. What had been the stabilizing hug of a busy schedule early in the month is now beginning to squeeze and hurt. I'm adding things to my to-do list as quickly as I check other things off. The ruling emotions are getting out of whack. It's not "love and joy come to you" but overwhelm and exhaustion. Although my impulse is to scramble harder, set even more ambitious daily goals, stay up later, and accomplish more, that still, small voice that may just be the voice of God is telling me it's time to do some paring down.

This is the time for a little Christmas honesty. That phrase itself may be a contradiction in terms, in that there's so much about Christmas or, at least, the way we've come to celebrate it, that is far from honest. Dressed up and sugarcoated. Adorned but not adored.

So how do we do the hard edit? How do we scrap plans and learn how to say no? With great difficulty, I'm afraid. Sometimes, our desire to create memorable Christmas traditions leads us to turn everything into a tradition, and the longer we live, the more layers of tradition accumulate. Traditions take on a life of their own and become important to other people. None of us like to let others down. But that same impulse not to let anyone else down is exactly the impulse that may have caused us to erect a teetering tower of impossible Christmas expectations. So how do we "de-tradition" and step back from some of the things that feel like chores and no longer deepen our sense of the season?

Remember, you *will* disappoint someone. I cringed as I wrote that last sentence. As a people pleaser, I live in mortal fear of letting other people down. Only lately, have I begun to understand that, sometimes, letting others down may be okay. Disappointing someone may help them take responsibility for their own happiness or find a better way of doing things. Your pulling out may set off a chain reaction that leads to a true reckoning, a long-overdue reality check. We all lapse into habits, and, sometimes, those near and dear to us need to have their habit of letting someone else organize their experiences be shaken up.

The people you let down may have meltdowns. They may not accept your backing off with understanding and grace. They may complain about your decision behind your back. They may try to guilt trip you. They may sulk or cry or give you the silent treatment. They may retaliate.

When you simply can't do it anymore, when you can no longer be the guardian, implementer, and clean-up crew for too many traditions, here are a few tips for letting others down gently:

#1 Do it early on. Don't be a coward and cancel at the last minute. The kinder thing to do is to give others a chance to make other plans or take on the task themselves. Give them the gift of time-liness and the opportunity to find alternatives.

#2 Offer a substitute, even a symbolic one. One year, someone who said she'd make some Christmas pageant costumes for me had to bail, but she gave me certificate at a fabric store. I still had to scramble to find a way to clothe the magi, but it did let me know that she wasn't just blowing me off, and that she had done what she had to do thoughtfully. Our relationship and respect for one another remains intact, decades later.

#3 Be vulnerable. Without overdramatizing things, explain why you have to back off. In a worthy relationship, this should deepen understanding. If you give someone a snapshot of your inner chaos, it's reasonable for them to respond with empathy, if not love. If they can't respond to your vulnerability, then maybe it was time to ease up on that connection anyway.

Letting people down is never easy, but we can try to do it with courage and grace.

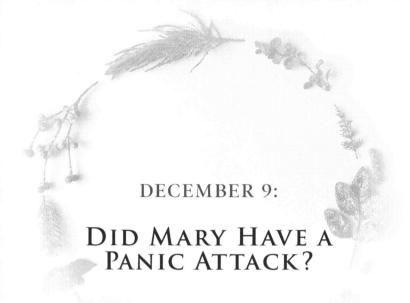

DECEMBER 9:

DID MARY HAVE A PANIC ATTACK?

The way the biblical story is usually presented is that a young and pregnant Mary goes off to visit her older cousin Elizabeth, who, as it happens, is also pregnant. We're presented with a picture of a symbiotic family support system, with the older and wiser Elizabeth offering guidance to the teenaged mother, and with the younger and presumably more energetic and agile Mary helping her kinswoman with the chores. A participant in a women's Bible study I once attended imagined cozy evenings of the two making baby clothes together. Generally speaking, the picture that is painted is one of Mary going to her cousin's house voluntarily and of the two women living together companionably for a good chunk of their pregnancies.

But the question that has always bothered me is how, in the hard scrabble economy of biblical Galilee, Mary's labor in her own household could have been spared? How could her family have afforded to let her go? Wouldn't they have needed her at home? Yes, she was pregnant, but she was young and fit and presumably not of a socioeconomic class where her labor would have been expendable.

Which makes me wonder if Mary got sent off to Elizabeth's for some other reason. Maybe they didn't know what else to do with her. What if all that pondering the Bible talks about meant that she was stunned into silence? Catatonic. Too overwhelmed to move through the normal rhythms of life. Maybe Mary was sent to Elizabeth's as a last resort. Perhaps they hoped that the older woman would ease her out of her stupor. Maybe they thought that the sensible, no nonsense Elizabeth could "do something" with her. Help her get her head screwed on right.

The idea of Mary suffering from panic attacks doesn't square with a strict reading of the biblical texts, nor with the portrait of Mary in the devotional tsunami that has followed over the centuries. Mary has come down to us as impeccably and impossibly serene. An exemplar of how we want to be as we sail not only through the Christmas season but through life itself.

But what if her pondering and her visit to Elizabeth's, while ultimately restorative, was born of her being overwhelmed and just plain shutting down? I would draw some comfort from that.

Because sometimes the Christmas juggernaut, in everything from its commercial to its spiritual ramifications, makes me want to shut down as well. At some point in my December journey, all the exuberance of the early days of creativity morphs into a sense of being overwhelmed. Sometimes, my body will be the harbinger. My back will ache. I'll wake up with a tickle in my throat. I'll start to feel especially lazy and skip exercising or shorten the walks that I take with my dog. I'll start to close down and close in.

When that happens, I may need to do what Mary did. I may need to find someone else to help me set the rhythms, to help me pace and pattern my days. If I'm lucky, this may happen in real time, with a real person, with someone as beloved to me as Elizabeth was to Mary. Can we spend the morning together? Or the day? Or maybe just a few minutes in between pick-ups, errands, and the other things that have to get done.

But when I'm Elizabethless, there are other ways to ease the panicky feelings, or that low-grade sense of distress, the anxiety of being overwhelmed. One is to pull back and take a wider view. Sometimes, it's just a matter of remembering all the Christmases that have come and gone, whether I was ready or not. Christmas is going to arrive, with or without anything I may contribute. And even at my best, the little bit of energy and mad perfectionism I throw into the Christmas game will be a drop in the bucket. Unnecessary in any cosmic sense. Unnecessary in all economies of grace.

Another tool is to fall into something easy, whatever "rote" means in our individual cases. It may be a chore or an activity or it may be going for a walk. Something that puts us in motion, but that doesn't require too much energy or thought.

In the Gospel of James, a gospel written around the same time as the more familiar biblical gospels, but one that never made it into the official canon, the angel visits Mary not once, but twice. A double Annunciation.

The first time, Mary is frightened by the news Gabriel bears and she retreats from the angel. The Gospel reports that she takes up her spinning, perhaps as a way of steadying herself as she tries to come to terms with what she's just learned. We see Mary going back to a repetitive household chore, something she can do automatically. We see a Mary who is very much like any of us. We may respond to unsettling news by throwing ourselves into a frenzy of cleaning or knitting or exercise or just getting in the car and driving around, something ordinary that doesn't require much thought.

Panicking at Christmas may have been part of the story right from the very beginning. We're in good company when we need to steady ourselves with a shoulder to lean on or with rote, mindless activity.

DECEMBER 10:

CHRISTMAS SEALS

Nothing derails the weeks leading up to Christmas like sickness. Even in families that enjoy good health, it's an easy time for immune systems to crash. Flu season may get served up early, colds and coughs are always on the menu, and for those with asthma, live Christmas trees can be an added challenge.

Illness and holidays often seem to intertwine. In my years of ministry, I have seen how unsettling it is for families when one of their loved ones is in the hospital as Christmas draws near. As one of my parishioners recalls, "Oh yeah, that was the year when I did all my Christmas shopping at the hospital gift shop."

However, the first time I connected illness with Christmas was when I was a girl and one of the coveted jobs in my family was putting the Christmas Seals on the cards my parents sent out. Christmas Seals are decorative stickers that can be purchased from charitable organizations and then applied to holiday envelopes in addition to the stamps required by the United States Postal Service.

Christmas Seals got their start in Scandinavia. In the early 20th century, before the advent of antibiotics, tuberculosis was a highly contagious and much feared disease. The prevailing treatment at the time was for patients to be sent away for months of rest at fresh air sanatoriums. These were expensive facilities to build and maintain, and there was always a scramble for funds. In 1904, a Danish postal clerk named Einar Holbøll came up with the idea of selling an additional stamp at Christmas time, and within just a few years, the sale of these stamps had raised enough money to build an impressive sanatorium.

A few years later, an American social worker, having read of the efforts in Denmark, decided to try the same thing, albeit it on a much smaller scale. Emily Perkins Bissell's goal was to raise $300 for a local institution in Delaware that was on the brink of closing. She designed the first seal herself, and although the initial sales were slow, the idea eventually caught on. The illustrator Howard Pyle, perhaps best remembered for his renderings of Robin Hood and King Arthur and often credited with having created the look we now associate with pirates, was an early contributor of artwork to his Wilmington neighbor's Christmas Seal effort.

Eventually, new drugs greatly reduced the threat of the disease and by the 1970s, the National Tuberculosis Society became the American Lung Association, still producing beautiful little embellishments to fight things like smoking, emphysema, and asthma. Over the years, the seals have featured Santas, snowmen, stockings, cardinals, puppies, mailboxes, wreathes, doves, drums, holly, and all manner of Christmas iconography. And in many instances, the Christmas emblems have been entwined with a subtitle—the word *Breathe.* It's all about being able to breathe.

During the holidays, it's all about taking the time to breathe. My friend, Tanis Frame (www.tanisframe.com), a self-described "play evangelist" whose mission is to help people (and women especially) to thrive, offers a simple exercise that she describes as life-changing for herself. When things feel like they're flying out of control (or even when they're not and you just want to reset the bar), Tanis advises that you STOP (right there, wherever you are), LOOK UP (stretch back your neck—gently of course—and look toward the sky), and BREATHE (in and out, you know how it works). Tanis, whose background is in the sciences, can tell you exactly why this is so effective at the neurological level, but I can attest that it does work. It's one of my go-to ways of regaining my composure when I'm under stress.

The Christmas Story in the Bible is full of people in stressful situations—women with heavy bellies, travelers competing for scant resources, people dealing with the unforeseen and the never before seen. I have to wonder if all that stress may have played with their immune systems the same way that holiday stress plays with ours. Maybe they could have used that same reminder to STOP, LOOK UP, and BREATHE.

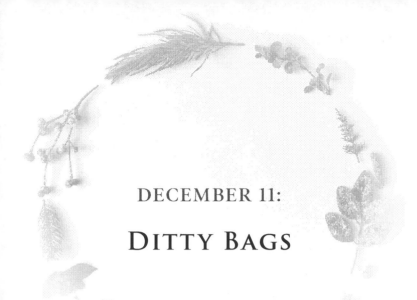

DECEMBER 11:

DITTY BAGS

At some point in December, I become a Grinch, at least for a day or two. This is almost always prompted by the "too muchness" of the season, the glut of food, decorations, experiences, music, performances, and other things to revel in. I get to the point where even a neighbor dropping by with the smallest gift, a single treat plopped in a brown paper lunch bag and tied with a piece of raffia can make me grumpy. *And now I have to come up with a way to reciprocate,* reads the thought bubble over my head. Sometimes I don't even recognize my own inner grumpiness until I start pushing away the things that would normally delight me. A normal response to such a gift might be, *Aren't I lucky to live in a neighborhood where neighbors know one another and do nice things for one another?* But December can skew my normal responses.

I was fortunate to grow up in a house where Christmas was celebrated without trauma and where there was a good balance of the spiritual, the social, and the material. We marched off to choir rehearsals and went to church. We performed various acts of December charity—boxing up personal items for prisoners, making stuffed animals for children at the New England Home for Little Wanderers, collecting canned goods and assembling the fixings for someone else's Christmas dinner. We had our own Christmas dinners with our grandparents and a bevy of great aunts, and we had neighbors who came by on Christmas morning. There was no alcohol to fuel any drama, and although there were the usual digs that family members can make, we were, on the whole, generally kind to one another.

Christmas presents were carefully chosen and always in plentiful supply. When I look at the slides my father took of our Christmas mornings, I'm shocked by just how many presents there were. What is also shocking is how few of the gifts I now remember. I'm sure I asked for things and received them, but it's hard for me to recall more than a few of the presents that I fervently hoped for and opened on Christmas morning, although I do know that I experienced the joy, the gratitude, and the sense of well-being that comes from getting what you most desire as a child.

Oddly, the presents that I remember best are the some of the humblest ones I received, the ones my great aunt Charlotte gave us. Charlotte never married and worked in low-paying housekeeping and food service jobs at the local hospital. She loved chocolate donuts, jigsaw puzzles, and lighthouses, and she lived to be 101. Every year, she would make my sisters and me ditty bags. She didn't own a sewing machine, so they were hand-sewn from cheap fabric she bought at the five and ten. All through the year she would collect little treasures to fill them with—free pocket calendars, American flag pins, bookmarks, crayons, small notebooks, Scotch tape, Elmer's glue, stickers, peppermints, and Quality Street toffees. There was nothing that we especially coveted or needed in Charlotte's ditty bags, but we loved her carefully curated collections, as well as the predictability of knowing that we would receive a new one every year. It was her signature gift. Nothing extravagant, but something she did with great love.

When I'm feeling the compulsion to shop more or when I start to feel that the things I've already acquired for my beloveds are not quite enough, I remind myself that the only gifts I really remember were modest. That less can be more and definitely more memorable.

DECEMBER 12:

GRIEVING FOR WHAT CANNOT BE

So much of Christmas is an act of imagination. Even those who would never call themselves creative crank up the imagination machine in December.

But the shadow side of imagination is grief. Because imagination can also conjure up the things that can never come to be. The things that exist in our own minds but never became real to anyone else. Some of these conjurings may be superficial—the projects we never got to, the gifts we never made, the cards we never mailed—but some of them are closer to the core. The reconciliations that never happened. The beloved ones who have abandoned us. The olive branch that never got offered. The family gatherings that we can look in on only in our imagination.

It may seem raw to put it this way, but, sometimes, Christmas can feel like a miscarriage in the sense that there are sacred dreams and visions we carry, that we are so bold as to allow to take root, but that simply cannot be brought to term. Maybe it's the dream of spending one more Christmas with our mother or father, or with the child we lost, or with the soldier who never came home. All the things that should have been but couldn't be.

Joni Mitchell's song "River" from her *Blue* album captures this mood. It's a melancholy tune about a breakup that happens at Christmastime.

It's coming on Christmas
They're cutting down trees
They're putting up reindeer
And singing songs of joy and peace
Oh, I wish I had a river I could skate away on.

While everyone else is enjoying the usual seasonal festivities, there is always someone who is feeling so out of synch that all they want to do is escape.

Sometimes, this melancholy may take a while to catch up with us. Sometimes, we're deep into the season before we acknowledge just what a grip it has on us. In some parts of the Christian tradition, the third Sunday of Advent is considered a Sunday of joy and is marked with lighting of a pink candle. Maybe this is the time for us to raise up a ritual of letting go. A blessing and a benediction, a farewell (or, at least, a placing on hold) to the things that cannot be or weren't meant to be, no matter how much we want them.

What would such a benediction look like? First, the acknowledgment of the part that did become real, if only to you: the seed, the kernel of promise, the hope. Pull out that jewel you held in your mind and hold it again. Honor it with wild tears and tender fury, and then try to lay it aside, at least for now. Put it in a safe place in your heart; for even if it didn't come to be, it's still yours. Still part of what makes you who you are.

And then, with words or without, try to celebrate one or two of the things that are coming into being. The new things that are wildly or shyly trying to be, waving at us or winking at us, trying to capture our attention, even as we grieve.

LULLABIES AND CRADLES

A wise elder, who passed through my life at exactly the right time, used to give new mothers a recording of lullabies, and if they had received some piano lessons along the way, a piano score of lullabies as well. But what made her wise was her claim that lullabies were for the mothers as much as for the babies. She knew from her own experience that often, the mothers needed the soothing most.

Lullabies do soothe. Neuromusicologists probably could tell us exactly what centers in the brain they fire up, but I suspect it has something to do with the simplicity of the songs. The rhythms are uncomplicated and propel us subconsciously into a rocking motion. The words often repeat, as in Silent Night, that most famous of all Christmas lullabies: *Sleep in heavenly peace, sleep in heavenly peace.* Given the pressures of the season, both in ancient Bethlehem and our own time, it's no wonder so many of the songs we associate with Christmas can be classified as lullabies or cradle songs.

Christmas supplies us with additional cradle imagery. In the late middle ages, miniature cradles for the Christ Child were popular devotional objects, especially in convents. Sometimes elaborate ones, gilded in silver or gold, were presented to women when they took their vows, and some medieval women participated in a performative kind of mystical devotion that involved rocking the cradle and mothering the Christ child in the form of a doll.

A friend of mine, who identifies herself as "never having been a doll person," surprised herself one December while out shopping for the gifts she donates each year to children in shelters. She was overcome by an uncharacteristic desire to buy dolls and doll furniture. "It was like I was possessed," she later reported. "All I could think about were baby dolls, cradles, and rocking chairs. And me, who only wanted skateboards and Nerf guns when I was growing up."

The desire to soothe and be soothed is part of the Christmas experience. It's grafted into the texts, songs, and spirit of the season. We live in a world where things are complicated and frightening. Yet we live with the promise that all shall be well, that all of the wants and injustices of our present knowing will be put to rest. The word *soothe* comes from an Old English word that means to 'show to be true.' To soothe, then, means to get at the truth of something, or to provide the comfort of truth to others. And wouldn't the authenticity and truth that all people yearn for be the very best Christmas gift we could give one another?

DECEMBER 14:

WHO'S COMING FOR CHRISTMAS?

One of the dances we perform during the month of December is the dance of figuring out who is going to spend what part of the Christmas holidays where. Which sibling is Mom going to stay with? Which year is it in the family-to-family rotation of the newlyweds? Is it too early in a relationship to count on spending the day together?

What we really need is a director or choreographer. Someone who would tell us where to go, how far to bend, and when to exit the stage. Someone who would relieve us of the need to work out the steps to the family dance on our own. There are so many ways in which these familial conversations break down. My own family has a decade old rift that best any of us can tell, began in a miscommunication over a holiday schedule. Of course, the issue ran much deeper, but a sense of exclusion in the making of holiday plans was the weakness in the surface of our family life from which toxic emotional lava erupted.

Sometimes, the frustration comes from different styles and rhythms of decision making. The branch of the family that wants everything nailed down early so they can buy tickets, make reservations, and piece together the rest of their master plan versus the branch of the family that likes to leave things open and sweep together a more spontaneous celebration closer to the end. In Myers Briggs typology language, the Judgers versus the Perceivers. The more ambitious the gathering, the more players, generations, and reaches of in-laws it attempts to include, the more complex all of this becomes. And, sometimes, it never does come together. Last year, it took my siblings and me an extra month to work out the details of our holiday gathering, an event we finally pulled off on Ground Hog Day.

Although that postponement wasn't what we intended, there is something to be said for offloading some of the season's festivities. They don't all have to happen during the month of December. One question to ask of anything that is causing anxiety during these hectic weeks is "Does this belong here? It is essential to do this during the month of December?" Messiah Sing, yes, because no one is going to mount one of those in February. As for visiting shut-ins (not your near and dear, but those random, do-good visits), why not plan it for a time of year when no one shows up? Like in the summer, when everyone is at the beach or heading out on vacation.

Working out plans with extended family takes patience, and even in the most loving and well-intentioned of families, it can introduce inadvertent stress. This is a good time to assess what the shape of the season needs to be like for you and what your boundaries are. Even if it's not your style, can you leave things open-ended? Or is there a drop-dead date by which you really, really need to know what's happening? And have you clearly and calmly communicated what you need to all players? Don't make them guess because, chances are, they'll guess wrong, and then you'll all be in a tailspin.

I do have a secret weapon in this overly complicated dance routine. And that is a fantasy of a perfect quiet Christmas, a solo performance instead of the ensemble work. What would my day be like if no one came to visit and I didn't go anywhere? Once you get past the expectations of boisterous houses filled with children, dogs, and other holiday guests, there's a certain deliciousness about a day of one's own. What would I eat? Listen to? Read? Watch? Would I paint, write, take a long walk, meditate, or do nothing at all? Would I sleep late or get up early? If there were not a single obligation, how would my Christmas day unfold?

That day will, no doubt, come for me, when my near and dear will be too busy or too far away or otherwise gone from this place. A time when my own Christmas Day will be depopulated. I'm not there yet, but I'm preparing myself for that eventuality, and I'm beginning to think it may not be so bad after all.

DECEMBER 15:

FEELING LONELY AT FAMILY GATHERINGS

I think there ought to be a Christmas demon. Some fierce, nasty creature that we could, in turn, tame by turning it into a Christmas ornament or icon of the season. Not an Elf on the Shelf, but a Devil on the Shelf. Dr. Seuss comes closest with the Grinch, but I'm thinking of something meaner and something more closely linked to our personal hauntings. Something that's not just bah, humbug, but boo, humbug. Something that would really scare us. In biblical terms, a Herod, that mass murderer who lurks in the background of the story of Jesus's birth.

Whether we admit them or not, we all have our Christmas demons. We all have memories of Christmases gone bad, Christmases that turned out to be lost opportunities (even though we didn't know it at the time),

Christmases when loneliness played through us as incessantly as Christmas musak at the mall. The Swiss have a word for the kind of loneliness that can settle in at Christmas time. *Weihnachtscholer*, they call it. It's the unhappiness that's even more keenly felt when everyone around us seems to be celebrating.

The worst kind of Christmas loneliness may be the version that occurs when you're surrounded by kith and kin yet cannot feel a part of them. All families build their own moats of values and assumptions, and even if they let down the drawbridge and welcome you, you still may not be wild about crossing over and entering in, even for a few hours.

There are countless sources of this interfamilial loneliness: being a political outlier; feeling that the acceptance of your partner is born of good manners, not genuine warmth; knowing that your children are being measured and judged; being chided for being too religious or not religious enough; feeling that, in their minds, you've been frozen in time and that the people around you are interacting with some prior version of yourself, not the person you've grown to be.

When we make Christmas Day (or the extended family gatherings at Christmas, whenever they occur) the pinnacle of the holiday season, we may be doing ourselves a disservice. Those gatherings may be something to get through, on a par with the winter concert at the elementary school, screechy violins included. They're something you can pat yourself on the back for having dutifully attended, but not the season's jewel in the crown.

Maybe the answer isn't to put all our eggs in the family gathering or Christmas Day basket. Don't expect those occasions to deliver what they can't. Just let them be minor Christmas moments and approach them with the expectation that they're not going to provide the full Christmas bang. We need to enjoy them for whatever they can deliver, whatever pleasantries, whatever reminiscing, whatever chance encounters happen to occur around the bowl of clam dip. My mother used to sing that old Doris Day song, *Que Sera, Sera,* and only now am I beginning to understand its wisdom. Whatever will be, will be. Accept things as they unfold. Sometimes, loneliness can be teacher. It shines a light on what's missing, on what matters, and on what we've come to need or hold most precious. When I was a kid, my family used to make fun of my bookishness. I was tagged as the one who "always had her nose in a book." The teasing stung, but through it, I came to realize how precious reading was to me. I couldn't wait for the relatives to leave so I could dive into whatever new books I had received for Christmas. While the easiest thing to do is to push those lonelinesses aside and distract ourselves with seasonal frivolity, sometimes, it pays to go deep and see what they're trying to tell us. We may not come through Christmas any happier, but it could bring us the gift of deeper self-knowledge.

DECEMBER 16:

THE PINK CANDLE

Sometimes it's the little things.

In the quasi-rural part of New Hampshire where I live, you either have to plan ahead or improvise. We try to consolidate our errands and make sure we have the things we need "laid in" ahead of time. Thus, the mistress of the candles at my church had, in due time, ordered a boxed set of Advent candles—three purples and a pink—and installed them in our Advent wreath. Low church as we are, we probably would have been fine with all white candles, but we had made the commitment to the purple and pink package, which has a nice symbolism to it. As Tsh Oxenreider sums it up, "the combination of one pink and three purple candles paints a portrait of Advent's overarching theme: sober anticipation mixed with a hint of joy."

And all was well, until the pink candle had an accident as the sanctuary was being cleaned and went down for the count. It was broken beyond repair. My ever-conscientious sexton informed me of its demise immediately.

But I forgot. The whole candle debacle slipped my mind until about 4 pm on Saturday afternoon, on the eve of the first Sunday in Advent. *But no problem,* I thought. *I'll just run into town and get a replacement.* At Thanksgiving, I had noticed a large display of candles at the stationary store and so I was confident that I could get the rose-colored one I needed.

But it's not the 1980s and dusty rose isn't a color featured in current home decor. So, there were no pink candles to be had. Not at the stationary store, nor at any of the other shops I tried.

I was getting crankier and crankier as it came on closing time. The only place left I could think of to try was the florist shop, which, of course, was crowded with families buying Christmas trees and evergreen roping and deciding what color bows to put on their wreathes. Finally, it was my turn, and when I explained my plight, the owner of the shop was immediately sympathetic. "I know!" he said. "Pink candles have been impossible to find this year. I've been trying to get some myself, but I can't even get them on special order." His ready commiseration made me feel better, but it didn't solve my problem.

I was almost out the door, when he said, "Wait a minute, let me try something." I followed him first to a workbench where he rummaged around for a can of spray paint, and then outside behind the store, where he took a white candle and coaxing the last bits of paint out of an almost empty can, spray-painted a hot pink candle for me. He refused to charge me for the doctored candle and shooed me along on my grateful way.

The candle was mottled if you looked at it closely, and as I was sitting in the big pulpit chair at the front of the church, I had a moment of panic the Sunday it was to be lit, wondering if spray paint was flammable and if it would flare up in some dangerous way. But as it turned out, there was no drama. No one in the congregation even noticed, until I told them the saga of the pink candle.

The third Sunday of Advent is called Gaudete Sunday in some liturgical traditions, *gaudete* being the Latin word for 'rejoicing.' The pink candle lit on this Sunday is meant to represent joy, and, that year, the makeshift one brought me extra joy. The joy of knowing that I live in a place where people are kind and generous and resourceful and really want to help you solve your problems, even the little ones. I want to be that kind of helper, too. Things that seem small to us may be of real consequence to someone else. If I can remember to keep looking for opportunities to do little things for others, it will be a good Christmas and a good life.

I SAW THREE SHIPS

Growing up, our repertoire of Christmas carols didn't come from a hymnal or a radio station playlist, but from a little booklet printed up and widely distributed (at least in the Boston area) by the John Hancock Insurance Company. We used the pamphlets in school and at Girl Scouts. Whenever we joined our neighbors caroling, someone always pulled out a box of them. The booklet was our Bible. It was shocking to learn later on that there were other carols, a canon beyond the fifteen indexed in Old English typescript on the back of the John Hancock booklet.

One of my later discoveries was "I Saw Three Ships Come Sailing In," an English folk carol, which, over the years, has become one of my favorites. It's the one I hum to myself every time I decorate our tree with the tiny ship ornaments we make out of walnut shells and the nautically themed ones we collected when we lived near Mystic Seaport.

But there's a spoiler in every crowd, and one Christmas, I got tripped up by a question someone posed about the carol's third verse:

O they sailed into Bethlehem,
On Christmas Day, on Christmas Day;
O they sailed into Bethlehem,
On Christmas Day in the morning.

Bethlehem, this exegete pointed out, is nowhere near the sea. That's true; Bethlehem is landlocked, a good forty-five miles inland.

Some say that the real legend behind this carol is about three ships bringing the relics of the magi to Cologne, Germany in the 12th century. The relics were so precious that they were placed on three separate ships, so if one went down, at least some of them would be preserved. In this version, the three ships represent caution and fierce protection.

During the Christmas season, we may find ourselves becoming uncharacteristically protective of our memories, our traditions, our time with our family, and a thousand other things that lurk just below the surface of our consciousness. The impulse to protect can be a good thing. It can make people feel safe, and in that place of security, give them space to shine and to thrive.

But protectiveness, particularly when it springs from those places that we're not fully in touch with, has a shadow side as well. It can exclude others, even when we don't mean to. It can make us reluctant to listen to new ways of doing things or to the voices of those who may have alternative ideas to share.

This season is a good time for us to inspect our own cargo and ask what's most precious to us and worthy of protection. But it's also a time to ask if we're protecting things that we ought to let go of, things that we no longer should be trying to bring into harbor.

DECEMBER 18:

STANDING IN LINE AT THE POST OFFICE

E very year, the United States Postal Service announces a date by which all packages must be mailed by in order to guarantee delivery in time for Christmas. In my little New Hampshire town, the post office is in the old Grange Hall. It has one window and one postal clerk, and closes for an hour at lunch. There's always a long line on that day.

There's a certain wistfulness on the faces of those who stand in line. Given the demographics of my community, a town that's aging and decidedly "silver," I would wager that a fair number of the packages are being sent to children and grandchildren in distant parts of the country. Children and grandchildren my good neighbors had perhaps hoped would come and visit this Christmas, but who, alas, have finally emailed or called to say, "not this year." Sally has a basketball tournament, the flights are too expensive, it's important for children to spend Christmas in their own home. Believe me, those of a certain age know all the reasons (or at least the stated ones) as to why their beloveds won't be able to make it.

On the appointed day, sneaking in just under the deadline, you'll find a long line of the newly and long retired who've done their best to put together a box that communicates all their love and hopes for generations living elsewhere.

It's hard to fit love, memories, and prophetic utterances into a priority mailing carton. Maybe it's one family's assortment of Christmas cookies, or an outfit to grow into, or a book about smart girls. We may send them reminders of the place they've come from. Here in New England, that can mean a jug of maple syrup, a Red Sox cap, a sketch of a chickadee scratched into birch bark, or a subscription to *Yankee* magazine. On Christmas Day, they'll call and thank us for these tokens (and for the checks that often accompany them), and although they're polite, well-raised children who know enough to effuse appropriately, we wonder if they really know. Do they know how much we love them and how much we miss them? Do the sentiments we try to cram into cartons really come through?

I wonder if that's how it is for God. God has sent so many messages over the millennia, so many gifts going out every millisecond, so many attempts to communicate that greatest of loves, but are we too busy, too distracted, too self-involved to properly receive them?

DESPITE THE RUINS
AROUND US

S hould I ever make it to Berlin, I'll probably go out of my way to hunt down a small nativity scene painting housed at one of the museums there. The work of art I want to see was painted five hundred years ago on a piece of linden wood and measures just 14 inches by 9 inches. It was painted by a German artist named Albrecht Altdorfer who was known for his forests, sunsets, and ruins. Altdorfer was one of the first northern European painters to take a serious interest in landscape.

Altdorfer's nativity shows Mary, Joseph, and the baby Jesus hunkered down in a set of ruins. You can see some timber framing, but vegetation is starting to take over what's left of the wooden structure. The Holy Family is sheltered from the wind by a brick wall that looks as if it might tumble at the touch. It's night, and except for a few cherubic angels and an ox munching away in the background, the Holy Family is all alone. Yet the desolate loneliness doesn't seem to be affecting the way that Mary looks at her child. Like mothers before and since, she gazes at him in wonder.

Dietrich Bonhoeffer mentioned this painting in a letter to his parents, written during Advent in 1943, when he was imprisoned at Tegel Prison by the Nazis. In the letter, he encourages his family to celebrate Christmas even more enthusiastically:

We can, and should also, celebrate Christmas despite the ruins around us...I think of you as you now sit together with the children and with all the Advent decorations—as in earlier years you did with us. We must do this, even more intensively because we do not know how much longer we have.

There are no perfect Christmases. Every Christmas has a bit of ruin to it, some more than others. Ruins may be uncomfortable places, but they're also picturesque. Some of our most memorable holidays are the ones that we've spent in "ruined" places where our expectations have collapsed or fallen down. Remember the year we had pizza for Christmas dinner because the pizza place was the only thing open near the hospital? Or the one when it snowed so much and the power went out, so we bagged the turkey and cooked hotdogs over in the fireplace?

Sometimes, graces are hidden in the ruins. As the Canadian poet/songwriter Leonard Cohen says in his song, "Anthem,"

There is a crack, a crack in everything
That's how the light gets in.

After the tears and sometimes even in the middle of them, ruins can generate laughter, connection, and a rich set of shared memories. Ruins can be sacred places.

DECEMBER 20:

MY SCARIEST CHRISTMAS EVER

I sometimes wonder what the percentage is of people who spend Christmas with something BIG hanging over their heads—a diagnosis, a break-up, a deployment. My scariest Christmas ever was the one I spent waiting for a stem cell transplant. After months of medical mystery and being kept alive (just) with blood transfusions, I had finally been diagnosed in November with multiple myeloma, a cancer of the blood plasma. It would take seven months of chemotherapy, steroids, and painkillers to get to the point of transplant, and, that Christmas, getting there wasn't a certainty. My blood counts weren't good, and it seemed plausible that the Christmas at hand might be my last, although we all tiptoed around saying that out loud.

I wasn't afraid of dying, but I was pretty worked up about the things that I thought I might miss. And perhaps more than anything else, I was filled with dread, deep-in-the-soul dread.

I dreaded the worry and uncertainty I was causing my mother, my children, and my congregation.

I dreaded going to the Dana-Farber Cancer Institute in Boston for a second opinion. I dreaded even crossing the threshold of that renowned institution because that was where my father had died of a different form of blood cancer some ten years earlier.

I dreaded not being of use. I had always been a side-by-side kind of minister, with an almost Benedictine, hearts-and-hands-to-God kind of spirituality. I worked alongside of people and we deepened our relationships that way. But my hands and my body weren't working. One day might be a good one, but the next, I might not be able to hold a cup of water or sit up or get myself dressed. I dreaded not being able to live in the world with any kind of physical predictability or the ability to lend a helping hand.

Likewise, I dreaded not being ready for what lay ahead. Would I have the grit and endurance? Surely, I had enough faith, will, and fight in me at the beginning, but would that still be intact six months down the road?

Would my faith, a faith I had spent my entire adult life proclaiming, stand up to the test? As a minister of the gospel, those stakes mattered to me more than any of the medical outcomes.

Henri Nouwen says that the more afraid we are, the harder waiting becomes. I would have given anything to have had some of that dread lifted off my shoulders that Christmas, but that's not how it works. Conquering dread is a little like sanding wood. You rub a little off at a time, smoothing as you go, sometimes imperceptibly.

One of the ways some of my own dread got sanded down during that time was with the help of my friend, Linda. Actually, she's more than a friend. My children and I refer to her as our family's guardian angel. Linda had picked up on my dread and decided that she was going to take charge and manage my trip to Dana-Farber. Guardian angels can sometimes be bossy, and I was too worn out and drug-addled to put up a fight.

First, she booked a room, a scandalously expensive room, at the best hotel I've ever stayed at. She arranged for a wheelchair, and, after a fireside lunch at the hotel bar, we toured Boston's Copley Square.

I've always loved Copley Square for its many beautiful buildings—the Boston Public Library, Old South Church, and impressive Trinity Church, an ornate building designed by Henry Richardson in the 1870s. A Saint-Gaudens statue outside of Trinity Church pays homage to one of its most famous preachers, Phillips Brooks. Although he was a prominent public figure in his own day, delivering the sermon at President Lincoln's funeral, today, he's remembered best for having written the words to the Christmas carol, *O Little Town of Bethlehem*.

We went inside Trinity Church, and on the eve of that much-dreaded visit to Dana-Farber, I opened up a hymnal and I saw something in the words to the familiar carol that I'd never noticed before:

Yet in thy dark streets shineth, the everlasting light.

The hopes and fears of all the years are met in thee tonight.

I've sung those words hundreds of times, but they struck me that day as new. I've always been trained to look up for God's light. I will lift up mine eyes to the hills. Follow the Bethlehem Star. It's always been about looking up for inspiration. I'd never thought of looking down. And certainly not down some dark street.

But that's the message I found that day sitting in Trinity Church and scanning the stanzas of *O Little Town of Bethlehem*. Sometimes, we have to look into dark streets, into the very heart of the things that fill us with dread. In my case, into this nasty blood cancer, into my anxiety about not being of use, and into my fear of not having enough faith to sustain me through the ordeal ahead. And sure enough, once I was ready to stare it down, there was a light shining in that dark street.

The faith I embrace (or more accurately, the faith that has somehow embraced me) is equal parts grit and mystery. It's a faith in which hope and fear are often intertwined. Over and over again, it seems to keep handing me tools for sanding down those layers of dread. A light that shines even in the dark places. A child who is always leading me to God.

DECEMBER 21:

IF I WERE AN ARTIST

When I go to the Agway store to buy dog food or dahlia tubers, I rarely seem to be able to resist the impulse purchase of one those miniature plastic animals on display near the cash register. That's how our nativity set acquired a turkey and a moose. While these examples of God's creatures dwell among us in my home state, it's a zoological stretch to think that they were ever part of the scene in Bethlehem.

However, I love the idea of mixing in a few outsiders at the manger. Yes, the sheep, oxen, and even the occasional dove we see in so many renderings of the nativity all hold their rightful place, but if I were a better artist, I'd paint a picture that included some of nature's less lovable animals. In an essay on British Christmas cards, the social anthropologist Mary Searle-Chatterje generates her own list of the animals that don't generally appear: bulls, porcupines, weasels, stoats, snakes, and large, predatory carnivores. I would add hyenas, nutria, bats, fire ants, cockroaches, feral cats, toads, pit bulls, skunks, jellyfish, rats, martens, fishers, and mountain lions—creatures we may fear, loathe, or just find peculiar.

Why do I want them there? I'm not entirely sure, but I think I want to know that there's room at the manger for the annoying and the ugly, and for the parts of me that bear those characteristics. When I'm prickly and shoot off words and thoughts that sting and bite, when the things I do for the sake of self-preservation are hurtful to others, when I act out of survival instincts rather than tenderness or thoughtfulness, I want to know that, even then, I'm still welcome at the manger.

Or maybe it's because I identify with the animals who've been left out. The ones not pretty or tame enough to be included. The summer after my fifth-grade year in school, my teacher (whom I adored) got married and invited a handful of girls from our class to her wedding: the photogenic ones with the nicest clothes who weren't too tall or too wide or already struggling with greasy hair and acne. You can probably surmise that I wasn't on the guest list. It stung at the time and made me distrustful of teachers for several years after that, but it did, at an early age, sensitize and seal my affinity with those who are left out of things.

So, if I were an artist, I'd paint a nativity scene that puts all of us there, the dull brown moths with broken wings, the gawky kids who haven't grown into their own bodies, the bullies with fear in their eyes, the dogs with three legs, even the black flies and mosquitoes. A painting that reflects how God might imagine the scene. A scene where we all belong.

DECEMBER 22:

BÛCHE DE NOËL

Years ago, in my days of culinary ambition (and during that era when we were all obsessed with Martha Stewart) I got it into my head that I wanted to make a Bûche de Noël to serve on Christmas Day. A Bûche de Noël is a rolled chocolate sponge cake shaped like a Yule Log. You make it in a jelly roll pan and then fill it with buttercream or a whipped filling, ice it in thick chocolate ganache, and decorate it with meringue mushrooms. Just before serving, you dust the whole thing with confectioner's sugar to give the impression of new-fallen snow. It's a show-off dessert and delivers enough sugar to put your guests in a coma for the rest of the Christmas afternoon.

I expected my Bûche de Noël to be a one-off. And the morning of Christmas Eve, my forearms smeared with chocolate and an uncooperative piping bag in hand, I vowed that this would be my first, last, and only attempt at such a ridiculously labor-intensive undertaking.

But my family had other ideas. By the following year, the Bûche de Noël had taken flight as the dessert "we always have" for Christmas dinner.

Children and adolescents can be fierce traditionalists, quick to turn something they've liked into sacred lore.

So, I kept making Bûche de Noël, through thick and thin. I squeezed it in during the Christmases that were rich and full of activity. I used it to fill time and anchor us during the ones that were ragged and hard to get through. I made small tweaks along the way. The quality of the chocolate got better over the years. And when we lost a family member whose favorite flavor combination was chocolate and orange, I dropped the Grand Marnier.

Recently, I learned that I could have saved myself hours of work over the years. As new partners entered the family, I heard my children describing our family's Christmas traditions to them. And after nearly three decades, I finally learned that it was all about the mushrooms. "The log's okay," I heard them say, "but what we really love are the meringue mushrooms. It wouldn't be Christmas without the mushrooms."

The mushrooms? The easiest and virtually foolproof part of the whole production? That's what it's been all about? Some year, I may call their bluff and skip the tricky rolled cake and the expensive chocolate ganache, and just serve up a platter of meringue mushrooms.

Maybe it's no surprise that the humblest part of our Christmas dessert extravaganza is the one that matters most. Christmas is always pulling us toward the humblest parts of things. A baby whose parents didn't even have enough clout to secure a room, never mind a good one. A Savior who came not as an eloquent prophet but as a teacher who conducted his business in the language of everyday things. Sometimes, great meaning attaches itself to the smallest things of all.

DECEMBER 23:

THE YEAR MY HUSBAND LEFT

My ex-husband left our family in November. There was no parting glass, no nod to what had been for twenty-three years, no leave-taking. I got word at a rest stop on the New York Thruway, a phone call that came through as I was driving to Toronto to find out just how sick our son was. He was calling to say that he had taken an apartment and hoped that we had enough money in the checking account to cover his security deposit and first month's rent. For reasons of his own, he chose not to tell us where this new apartment was located. I had known that our marriage was in trouble, although I had yet to understand the full breadth of the reasons why. But what I knew immediately was that the life I had known was over. I wasn't going to celebrate any of the big anniversaries or sit beside him at our daughter's college graduation. Since we were on staff at the same church, I wasn't going to be able to continue in a ministry I loved. Even my understanding of myself as a mother was suddenly on shaky ground, so entwined had it become in our identity as co-parents.

As that sad Christmas approached, one that I knew would be my last one in a house I loved—a Craftsman style bungalow with a wide front porch, a bank of pink phlox at the curb, and figured gumwood paneling that looked like elves in the dining room—it was all I could do to go through the motions. I had found a part-time job in a museum across the border in Massachusetts, and it took everything in me just to get there and back. When I got home, I would heat up a can of tomato soup and crawl under a quilt that one of our former parishioners had made for us. I watched a strange combination of television programs—the *Suzie Orman Show,* the *Travel Channel,* and re-runs of old family comedies, all of which made me feel worse than I already did. I didn't have enough money, I would never travel, and my identity as a parent was coming apart at the seams. I wish I could say that I cried and sobbed and raged. But I was too numb even for those normal responses.

Instead, I hid and worried and fantasized. I imagined that Christmas would reconcile our family. That my children's father would turn up on Christmas Day and we would, of course, open the door and welcome the prodigal home. Which is exactly what didn't happen. It was a Christmas of absences, both around the table and under the tree. I had presents for the kids, but they were meager. And all of the extras that our former congregation had provided for us fell away. No one dropped off a poinsettia. There was no basket of fruit, no Christmas bonus, not even the annual gift box of Turkish Delights, pasty fruit jellies that we never could decide whether we liked or despised. It felt odd not going to church on Christmas Eve. It felt odd ordering Chinese take-out instead of cooking a proper Christmas dinner. It felt odd trying to tiptoe around our old traditions. If I could have, I would have traveled to my sister's house and regrouped there, but she lived four states away, and I had to be at work on the day after Christmas.It was as sad as even this abridged description makes it sound, in many ways, a broken, pathetic holiday. But that was also the Christmas that turned the tide. And the one thing, the one memory I have of that Christmas morning, was the way my son wrapped his gift to me. I can no longer remember what the gift was, but it was wrapped in a way that may have saved my life. My son Nat, who is always inventive in his presentations, had taken an old box that a Playmobile set had come in and he had used an Exacto knife to carve out six-inch letters that were folded until they stood upright from the box. "MA" they spelled out. I may have felt like I had lost every other part of my identity, but I was still his Ma. Over time, many of the things that I thought I had lost would come back to me, and more than a few unimaginable blessings have turned up in my life. But that long recovery and discovery of self began that Christmas morning. Stripped of everything else, I was still my son's Ma.

Christmas that year was a wisp of its former self and as fragile as a cobweb, but it surprised me with a few drops of undiluted joy. And joy, even in the tiniest of quantities, is what heals us.

DECEMBER 24:

SHEDS AND STEEPLES

My church is one of those classic New England meetinghouses—white clapboard with a tall steeple and Palladian windows. It's the kind of building you see on photo calendars and jigsaw puzzles, and thanks to a whole roster of dedicated townspeople, it's the kind of building that wins architectural preservation awards.

But what makes my church unique are the horse sheds out back. They're substantial—a long, gracefully curved series of attached sheds, set on a stone foundation and roofed in slate. They aren't as old as the church, but still date back to the 19th century. Built by a local carpenter, they were designed as part of a beautification project by the same landscape architect who laid out the grounds for the Breakers mansion in Newport,

Rhode Island. This is pretty fancy stuff for a rural New Hampshire town.

However, our ancestors were clear about what the stables were for. On Christmas Eve in 1895, they voted that no one could occupy a shed for the purpose of storage to the exclusion of anyone who wanted to use it to stable a horse. Animals first. There's something very grounded and sensible about a community where sheltering animals is one of its prime concerns. This is still a town that loves its animals. We often know the names of people's dogs, long before we learn the names of their human companions. The award-winning author Sy Montgomery has written about how the whole town embraced her pig Christopher Hogwood, in her memoir, *The Good, Good Pig.*

But the horse sheds have a companion: the meeting-house steeple. Soaring by local standards, it's the town's only highrise. A resoundingly impractical and expensive embellishment (as the generations who have taken care of it will attest), it rises above the horse sheds, directing our eyes vertically to the heavens, keeping us, we hope, in a heavenly frame of mind. Its purpose is to elevate and inspire.

Something that grounds us and something that elevates us. Sheds and a steeple. A perfect pairing. And the pairing we find in the Christmas Story. Because if we walk around to the backside of the Christmas Story, and look at it from a certain distance, we find it's a story defined by two things—one born of earth and one born of heaven.

It's a story about starlight and straw. The ethereal, inspiring starlight that brings us to the manger but also the straw, the humble, earth-grown, bedding material, the sweetest and best on offer when it was time to cradle the baby Jesus.

Just as divinity and humanity become one in the child born at Bethlehem, our best selves—our Christmas selves—are ones that look up to God for inspiration, but then live out what we've seen in the starlight on much humbler ground, amongst the straw and sweat and toil of daily life, amongst the hard work of caring for others.

Some families practice a French custom, I'm told, of putting out an empty manger at the beginning of Advent and placing a little pile or bag of straw next to it. Every time someone in the family does a good deed or something to help another person, every time someone tells the truth under difficult circumstances or does something brave, a single piece of straw is placed in the manger. The object, of course, is to fill the manger by

Christmas Eve, so that when the figure of baby Jesus is laid there, he'll rest comfortably on a plump bed of straw.

It's a lovely custom, but the good deeds that faith demands aren't time-stamped with an expiration date that runs out on December 25. Good deeds aren't seasonal. The baby Jesus needed someone to fix him a bed of straw, but the world is still full of other children, children of God whatever their age, who need protection and shelter and a safe place to rest. We may be inspired by steeples and starlight, but our real work is out in the horse sheds, in all the practical places where God's creatures need our care.

DECEMBER 25:

CHRISTMAS MORNING CHAOS

When my father died, he left behind ten steel boxes of Kodachrome slides, mostly pictures he took of our family between 1956 and 1978. These have corrected some of our memories, supplemented others, and in general, provided our family with lots of fodder for conversation.

One of my father's favorite subjects was the chaos of Christmas morning. There are very few pictures of his three girls neatly posed in the Christmas dresses we would change into in time for our grandparents' arrival later in the day. However, there are plenty of us taken early on Christmas morning, with startling cases of bedhead and hastily thrown on housecoats, grinning amid mountains of wrapping paper debris.

We weren't a tidy, clean-up-as-you-go kind of family. My parents operated free style. Presents would be handed out, paper would be pulled off and dropped, eventually piling up around us and covering the living room floor. Sometimes, instructions and even small pieces of gifts would get lost. Often, things got stepped on.

Maybe, in reaction to this level of disorder, I ran a different kind of ship on Christmas morning when I got to be the adult in charge. I wince now when I think of myself walking around with a garbage bag or sitting on the sidelines with a clipboard, dutifully recording notes about each gift as it was opened so that we would have an accurate list when it came time to write thank you notes. All very orderly and controlled but, truth be told, not much fun.

It's a conceit to think that anyone can really manage Christmas the way I once tried to. Both in the biblical story and in our own living out of the day, there's just too much in it for us to be in charge of, too much to process and appreciate. There's no way to bundle and record all of the expectations, intentions, and dreams that are wrapped into our celebrations. In any given go at it, there will be parts of it that we'll miss, parts of it that we'll inadvertently discard, and parts of it that will get lost.

Yes, I want to hold onto as much of it as I can, but I also want to live in the moment and be that little girl in my father's slides, the one with the big smile and the hair standing out on end, who seems to know something I later lost track of, at least for a while. She knew, and I'm rediscovering, that Christmas happens in the moment. That's where the joy is.

Merry Christmas!

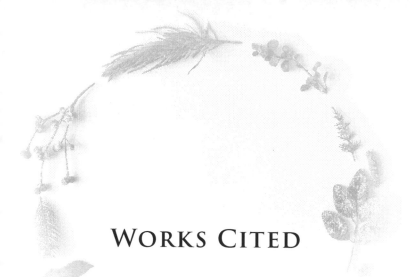

WORKS CITED

Bonhoeffer, Dietrich. *Dietrich Bonhoeffer's Christmas Sermons.* Edited and translated by Edwin H. Robertson. Grand Rapids: Zondervan, 2005.

McEntyre, Marilyn. *Making a List: How a Simple Practice Can Change Our Lives and Open Our Hearts.* Grand Rapids: Eerdmans, 2018.

Oxenreider, Tsh. *A Simple Advent Guide*, 2017. www.tshoxenreider.com.

Searle-Chatterje, Mary. "Christmas Cards and the Construction of Social Relation in Britain Today." *Unwrapping Christmas.* Ed. Daniel Miller. Oxford: Clarendon Press, 1993.

ACKNOWLEDGMENTS

I am grateful to my late parents, who gave my siblings and me such beautiful Christmases as children. I am also grateful to my own children, who, later on, gave me the chance to try my own hand at Christmas making. Thank you for the silliness and joy, and for your faithful presence in the balcony on Christmas Eve.

Thanks go to my dear friend Linda Lutfy-Clayton and my sister and brother-in-law, Joanne and David Rodgers, for being the loving, generous, and upbeat people that they are. Thank you for always being there for me.

I am also grateful to the congregations that have, in so many ways, been Christmas laboratories for me over the years. Thank you for teaching me your traditions and for allowing me to experiment with a few of my own. Beginning with congregations in Woodbridge and Norwichtown, Connecticut, and then the First Congregational Church in Manchester, New Hampshire, and finally, the Hancock Congregational Church, I have been blessed to be among you for so many Advent and Christmas seasons. In particular, I owe a debt of gratitude to the members of the Hancock Church for providing me with sabbatical time to write this book and for supporting the Monday Meditation sessions during Advent where some of these ideas made their debut.

Thanks also to Gary Williams and Wayne Purdin for their encouragement and technical assistance, and for their help in keeping the sometimes arduous process of bringing a book into the world going.

And finally, I am grateful to my oncology team—Steve Larmon in New Hampshire and Ken Anderson and Tina Flaherty at the Dana-Farber Cancer Institute—for their knowledge, devotion to the art of healing, and faith in me as a patient. Thank you for this precious extra time.

Judy Copeland
Hancock, New Hampshire
August 2019

ABOUT THE AUTHOR

Judith Copeland is a writer and United Church of Christ minister. Raised just north of Boston, she has served churches in Connecticut and New Hampshire for over thirty years. She graduated from Dartmouth College, earned her M.Div at the Harvard Divinity School, and is also a juried member of the League of New Hampshire Craftsmen. Judy has a daughter and a son, two grandchildren, and a rescue dog named Lily. She lives in Hancock, New Hampshire where she draws inspiration from her view of Mount Monadnock, her garden, and her congregation at the Hancock Congregational Church.

Connect with her online at judithcopeland.com and on Instagram @jcnh.

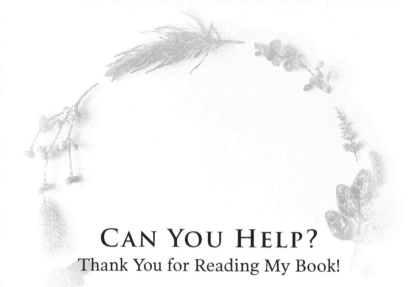

CAN YOU HELP?
Thank You for Reading My Book!

I really appreciate all of your feedback, and I love hearing what you have to say. I need your input to make the next version of this book and my future books better.

Please leave me an honest review on Amazon letting me know what you thought of the book.

Thanks so much!
Judy Copeland

Made in the USA
Monee, IL
23 December 2019

19480675R00070